ELEVEN GLORIOUS DAYS

by

Mark Schlitt

I0789182

Content

<u>PROLOGUE</u>

Mention backpacking and many people mistakenly think of camping or hiking. However there are major differences between backpacking, hiking and camping that deserve an explanation.

The dictionary defines **camping** as, "to live temporarily outdoors, in a tent or camper usually for recreation". When we think of camping, we conjure up images of loading the kids, a tent and every material comfort we can fit, into the car, station wagon, mini-van, SUV, or even RV, and heading off to a campsite in the "Great Outdoors". The vehicle used is an integral part of the camping experience in order to bring all the conveniences of home with us while we're "roughing it". Huge tents, camp stoves, pots and pans, coolers filled with ice and food, and even television sets and video players, are not uncommon on camping trips. Computers, cell phones, iPads or other tablets and devices are necessities in order to amuse the kids, play video games, stay in touch with friends and family, and post to social media so everyone back home knows how much fun *we* are having and what *they* are missing. If a lake is part of the camping experience then we can add boats, jet skis and any number of other fun water toys.

The vehicle is the pantry, refrigerator, closet but also the means of escape to the movies or out to dinner if the designated chef burns it, blows it, drops it in the fire or ashes (or just turns out to be a "chitty chef") or the desire for pizza or ice cream arises. It's also the method of rescue from rain or snow, cold or heat, wind or nasty bugs, or in the unfortunate event someone becomes sick or is injured. Camping is simply transferring as many of the luxuries of home to a place near a lake or stream and trees to experience "country living" or the "Great Outdoors". To perfectly illustrate that concept, a recently coined word "glamping" combines the words glamorous and camping for those who can't live without the luxuries of home while enjoying the benefits of camping.

Hiking is simply defined as "the activity of going for long walks, especially in the country or woods". It can involve a short time or distance, or longer excursion, but is typically considered an experience done in one day. Consequently, a day pack or knapsack is all that is needed to carry lunch or snacks, water or drinks, bug repellent or sunscreen and maybe a poncho or jacket in case of rain or change in temperature. Hiking can be part of a camping experience depending on the goals of the trip and whether trails are nearby to explore. Hiking is also an activity not involving camping at all, such as a short hike in the woods to bird watch, or simply enjoy the beauty of nature, or to reach an off road stream or lake.

Backpacking is a horse of a different color entirely and can be broken into several general categories listed below.

1. Short trips, typically 4 days or less.

2. Long trips, longer than 4 days.

3. Trips along heavily traveled trails where camping is only allowed in designated camping areas along the trail. Reservations of individual spots within each camping area are required due to the large number of backpackers. This type is most commonly found in busy National Parks or popular hiking trails, such as parts of the Appalachian Trail. On the bright side, these camping spots normally have some amenities such as outhouses and water.

4. Trips along level terrain with minimal elevation changes.

5. Trips in mountainous areas in high elevations and with large elevation changes.

6. Destination trips consist of packing everything to a specific location where a camp is set up and day hikes are made from the camp to other locations. The advantage here, is that the day hikes are much easier since most of the heavy gear is left at camp each day.

7. Wilderness backpacking. As the name suggests, the trip takes place in a wilderness area where there are few people, no amenities, but potentially an abundance of wildlife, and plenty of solitude and peace and quiet.

Backpacking trips require in-depth planning and preparation prior to the trip, and discipline and ingenuity during the trip. With backpacking, the vehicle is simply a method of travel to and from the location where the trip begins. Upon departure the automobile is left behind and the method of travel becomes the backpacker's feet and legs. On a backpacking trip of a week or longer, the distance traveled can easily be 100 miles or even much more. During the trip, everything needed for survival must be carried with the backpacker. All protective clothing, food, sleeping bag, tent, utensils, stove, water filtering devices, first aid kit, and anything else that might be needed for survival during the entire length of the trip must be carried by the backpacker for the duration of the trip. Backpacking means trekking over rough terrain, in some areas up and down steep mountain trails with elevation changes of thousands of feet while carrying 50 plus pounds of life-sustaining items. Weather conditions of rain, sleet, snow, hail, lightning, strong winds, and blistering sun, along with temperatures ranging from near freezing or below, to sweltering heat can be experienced on one trip. The clothing and protective gear needed for survival and comfort must be included even if never used. With all the gear required, weight is a major consideration. Creative and innovative weight-saving ideas are critical to a successful trip. Freeze dried packaged meals are an excellent way to save weight since food is the heaviest single item that also takes up the most space on any trip. Some experienced (or should we say fanatical?) backpackers go as far as removing the cores of toilet paper rolls to save weight. Some people rent llamas to carry their food and gear. Although llamas may solve the weight problem they also limit the time and location of a trip since pack llamas aren't universally available.

Food for a trip of more than a week is another major dilemma. A trip of 11 days requires planning between 22 and 33 meals plus numerous snacks with weight, nutrition, caloric needs and taste all taken into account. Planning and preparation are critical. On a trip where someone develops diarrhea, the danger of running out of toilet paper is no laughing matter (as we all laugh at the thought). Underestimating the importance of this simplest item, until faced with the reality of taking care of business (yes, pun intended) without it could ruin a trip. Minor inconveniences in normal daily life, become major problems when backpacking. Think blisters, especially on the feet, since the feet are your transportation, or sunburn, when sun, especially at high elevation can cause headaches, pain and even severe skin damage.

Consider also, that five days into an 11-day backpacking trip, if you're tired and want to go home, want to talk to the family, want a pizza and cold drink, or simply want to call it quits, with the car five days away none are viable options. Camping trips are for outdoor lovers and attention to detail will result in a more enjoyable experience. Backpacking is for the outdoor fanatic where details and preparation mean the difference between pain or pleasure and, in severe circumstances, even life or death.

CHAPTER ONE

Begin With Family

Almost every backpacking trip is memorable, but eleven days in the Gila Wilderness of New Mexico was beyond all hopes and expectations. This trip began by "grandpa" (that's me) meeting two daughters, two grandkids and a special son-in-law in New Mexico for the first 3 days. The kids and grandkids live 17 hours and two visits per year away. Whenever we get together it's (you know the story) never long enough. It was the grandkids (ages 7 years and 4 months) and oldest daughter's first backpacking trip. Unfortunately, it was also the rainiest 3 days of the year. Poor 7 year old TaLora thought she was going to be washed away while riding on grandpa's shoulders crossing the rain-swollen mountain creek. On the third day after packing up and hiking back to our vehicles, while saying our good-byes, most said they had a good time and wanted to do it again. Then grandpa went back into the wilderness for eight more days. This is the story of the eleven glorious days.

<u>CHAPTER TWO</u>

Beginning Transformation

I drove back up into the mountains on the steep, winding dirt road past the old ghost town of Mogollon. The "town" of Mogollon was built starting back in the late 1800s by miners who found silver and gold in the area. My mind was racing, thoughts split between the recent experiences of the last three days and the anticipation of what the next seven to ten days alone in the wilderness would bring. I pulled into the over 9,000' elevation trailhead area where three trails headed in different directions, and parked as far away from the two vehicles as possible. Only two vehicles was a good sign since I liked not seeing strangers when hiking alone.

I had once asked a Park Ranger on horseback I crossed paths with while backpacking in Yosemite National Park if he carried his sidearm for protection from bears or mountain lions. His response surprised me and I never forgot it. He told me animals were predictable and there were none he feared, but wilderness areas occasionally attracted bad guys who wanted to do bad things to unsuspecting, innocent victims where there are no witnesses and they can get away with almost anything. Even though I have never had a bad experience with strangers while backpacking, his testimony, combined with several gruesome examples I've read about over the years, has made me super cautious when traveling alone.

I ambled over to the outhouse to use the "civilized facilities" for probably the last time in a long while. Under normal circumstances most people would avoid using this facility or use it only in an emergency, but right now, to me it was a luxury, an enclosed, private place to sit, out of the weather, in moderate comfort. Never mind the odor, the flies and other creatures crawling around, or the fact that there was no water. It was the best I would see in quite a while.

After finishing job number two, I went back to my vehicle and started organizing my pack for the trip, but the rain, though intermittent, was heavy enough to keep me in the vehicle. The worst way to start a trip is with wet clothes, sleeping bag and gear. The darkness was fast ending my chances of getting a start today, so I gave in to the idea of sleeping in the car. It's difficult to sleep soundly in a car especially with nature's splendor beckoning, but morning came soon enough and the beauty of the red, orange and purple streaks in the sky told me I had made the right decision. The dreary rain clouds were gone, replaced by blue sky and appealing white fluffy puffs drifting slowly by. An hour later my 80 pound pack was organized and on my back. My belly was full, the "luxurious" outhouse had been used one last time and I was on my way up the trail with 75' tall white bark Aspens, 100' tall ponderosa pines and stately old Douglas fir framing the magnificent scene.

Deep, abiding and complete peace, plus the magnificent beauty of every detail of nature assaults the mind and the senses within minutes. The worries of the normal day melt away. The aggravation of ringing phones, to-do lists and deadlines disappear. Concerns of how to satisfy the boss's demands, the financial squeeze and everyday problems move to the background or vanish temporarily. The bombardment of wailing sirens, chattering televisions and radios, barking dogs, noisy trucks and other vehicles is replaced by the whisper of wind through the leaves of the trees, the chirping and singing of birds, the hum of birds' wings, the babble of streams, and the buzz or twitter of small animals and insects. Soothing sounds normally silenced by the screams and demands of society emerge to be enjoyed. Within moments of beginning a wilderness adventure I always decide I must do this more often. Tattered nerves are calmed. Rushed petty thoughts of perceived importance are swallowed and trivialized by the surrounding grandeur of distant mountain peaks, forests, colorful flowers and flowing streams. Where complex issues and problems once consumed and enslaved, here simplicity enlightens and empowers. Though mere minutes are needed to recognize the beginning of one's transformation, days are required to advance the process for indelible, noticeable change.

I moved steadily away from the parking area where my vehicle allowed almost complete control of my environment, to suffer neither cold nor heat nor rain and the ability to access food to satisfy any desire, or entertainment for any whim practically instantaneously. In this new environment my survival and comfort depended on my wits, the equipment I carried and nature. The challenge was exhilarating, almost intoxicating. Some people fear, abhor and shy away from challenges. Others don't feel truly alive without experiencing frequent challenges and tests.   They have to know they are capable of rising above difficulties, performing under pressure or beating the odds. For these people it is as necessary as breathing to be frequently pushed to their limit and beyond.

As I moved deeper into the wilderness I began to take notice of the creatures whose domain I was invading. The birds and small animals enjoyed the puddles the rain had left behind. It never failed to amaze me how wild animals adapted to whatever nature had up its sleeve, while it often caused me great discomfort. I snickered at the vision of a chipmunk needing a backpack filled with nuts, berries and raincoat as he frolicked from puddle to tree.

Each step worked out my body's kinks after a night in the car. The cool damp air felt invigorating since I was dry and warm. Another hour up the trail and my sweatshirt and sweat pants came off leaving me in the ideal clothing of hiking shorts and t shirt. The sun felt warm and soothing against my skin while the gentle breeze was refreshing and cooling. In this moment life was as perfect as it could be. Moving steadily, heart pumping, breathing deeply from the pleasant exercise, sweat lightly dripping, enjoying the sights, sounds and smells, every turn revealing new wonders. No schedule, no deadlines to meet, no one to answer to, I felt totally at ease and in complete control. Even whether this would be a five day or ten day trip was within my purview. The freedom was intoxicating.

CHAPTER THREE

History And Questions

Glimpses of dates, names and information carved into the bark of the tall old Aspens entertained me for miles. The older the carving the higher up the tree and the less legible the words and numbers appeared. Occasionally I would stop to examine the details of a particularly interesting specimen. The names and dates back to the mid 1900s were still easy to read, while the dates back to the early 1900s had become more difficult due to tree growth stretching them and weather eroding them. The idea that some of these magnificent trees were large and sturdy enough seventy, eighty and even ninety years ago for someone to inscribe their names for future travelers to see was intriguing. For miles I was lost in a time warp imagining what the roads were like, what the forest looked like, and what shoes and clothing these nearly century old travelers wore. Did Tom who loved Mary enough to tell all passers, stay together till death did them part? How old were they when they inscribed those impetuous words and how long did they live after their inscriptions? Did they have children who inherited their love of nature or who even came to see where dad immortalized his love for mom? The stories these trees could tell, if only they could tell.

The sky transformed from one hour to the next. Clear, cloudy, dark, then rain, at which time I would hurry to get my poncho over my pack and rain slicker over my body to protect both from the weather. Majestic, powerful lightning, could be frightening and in remote mountainous areas could be extremely dangerous.

Being struck by lightning may be rare, but more common while hiking or backpacking than most would imagine. I had just summited Mount Whitney days before my birthday in July 1990 when a storm suddenly blew in and our group rushed for lower ground. Tragically, the thirteen people who made the summit shortly after we left were struck by lightning resulting in one death and numerous injuries. A lesson so close and traumatic isn't easily forgotten.

The rain contained hail occasionally, then the storm blew away and the sky once again became bright and friendly. Poncho and slicker were then tied to the pack to dry, ready for the next rainy spell. The miles and hours flew by as I approached Hummingbird Saddle at around 10,500' elevation. Having taken several side trips and numerous stops to investigate items of interest and satisfy my curiosity, I was only 7 miles up the trail and it was already early evening and time to find a good spot to camp for the night. When traveling alone I usually camp far enough off trail to be hidden from any hikers moving up or down the trail. This evening I decided to build a fire to save propane for the rest of the trip, but the previous heavy rains had soaked every scrap of tinder and wood nearby. I considered myself an expert at building a fire often boasting that if it took more than one match you must be a novice. But this night, even after an hour long battle, smoke and small flames that quickly extinguished were my only rewards. This meant pulling out the pack stove, a change of menu and another 30 minutes to accomplish something as simple, but as necessary as dinner. Ordinary things taken for granted and accomplished in mere minutes at home could become major time consuming tasks alone in the wilderness. It was totally dark when I finally settled into my sleeping bag. Cleaning utensils, organizing my camping area and backpack and protecting it from rain were an important nightly chore. I thanked God for His undetected presence and protection as was my custom and thought of the words penned thousands of years before, "The Lord is my shepherd, I shall not want". The words had far more meaning for me, alone, under the dark and threatening sky. I was indeed at His mercy, but the words of King David were a definite comfort as I drifted off to a sound sleep probably not far from mountain lions and bears.

I was awake before first light but enjoyed lying quietly in my warm sleeping bag listening as the day's symphony began playing while watching the living painting being created before me. The sky grew from dark to light with colors splashing to life in every direction. The tall dark shadows slowly became white and brown giants shooting straight from the ground to the sky, massive towers of strength waving their green appendages in the breeze. A shiver crept up my spine as I contemplated my puny insignificance in the total picture. Any one of these magnificent ponderosa pines, which reached heights of well over 100' and weighed dozens of tons, dwarfed me physically in every respect. I was in a forest surrounded by thousands, if not millions of trees, a mere speck in the scheme of things here and the thought was humbling.

Today's hike included Mogollon Baldy Peak and the Forest Service Lookout Tower, but from there I hadn't decided which direction to go. The problem was my topographical maps didn't cover the area I might want to explore. It was a troubling thought to be entering an unfamiliar area without good detailed maps. As always, I was confident this dilemma would resolve itself satisfactorily before a final decision had to be made.

CHAPTER FOUR

Surprise Surprise

The trail from Hummingbird Saddle turned east amid a dense spruce-fir forest. A mile down the Crest Trail an interesting looking side trail veered off to the left. I stashed my pack behind a tree off trail, filled my belt canteens with water from bottles in my pack, grabbed a few snacks and took off down Iron Creek Lake Trail. A few hundred yards down the trail I noticed a steep drop off on the right, and decided to investigate. Since I was wearing shorts I navigated through the trees and brush slowly to avoid scratches and cuts to my legs. As I came near the cliff's edge, the trees thinned and it became brighter. A few steps from the cliff's edge, a loud noise erupted immediately in front of me. I jumped, startled to see an enormous golden eagle fly past my head. The "Hoop Whoop" noise from its wings was far louder than I ever could have imagined. From the distances I normally saw eagles, they appeared to silently soar through the sky or float effortlessly overhead. Up close in the peaceful, silent environment and totally unprepared for the event, this one sounded as loud as a helicopter. I wondered whose heart was beating faster, the beautiful, majestic eagle's or mine since I apparently startled the huge, amazing creature as much as it surprised me. It was a great lesson regarding

my ignorance of the many splendors of nature.

I went back to the trail and followed it a little further until I saw a field

filled with some unusually beautiful purple and yellow wild flowers. The trail

was becoming steep and difficult to follow due to overgrowth and lack of use.

When I finally stopped to turn back, the trail was still abnormally steep ahead.

The further I proceeded on this trail the more difficult would be the journey

back to my backpack. One canteen was dry already and there was no sign of

water anywhere so I started back up toward Crest Trail.

Several miles later it was slow going as the Crest Trail rose steadily

higher toward Mogollon Baldy. The area abruptly changed from heavily

forested to new growth smaller trees. This was obviously the site of a good

sized forest fire not too many years previous. The trail began to zigzag back

and forth in switchbacks as it got steeper and on both sides it was filled with

blackberry plants that were loaded with delicious ripe wild fruit. I devoured as

many of the ripe irresistible berries as were within reach. What a treat the

sweet, juicy, luscious, dark purple and black balls were. Fresh, wild

blackberries were not part of my normal everyday life back home so I savored

the experience, enjoying each one. They were soft and juicy with a unique,

perfectly delicious flavor and texture. I held one close to my nose and enjoyed

its delicate aroma, popped it into my mouth and rolled it around for a few

seconds before squeezing it between my teeth. The sweet juice oozed onto my tongue, combined with the slightly rough texture of the fruit, creating a symphony of taste enjoyment. Oh the simple unexpected pleasures of life. Here, where all the food in my pack was freeze dried and packaged to save weight, these nuggets were an amazing, unexpected joy and delight.

CHAPTER FIVE

Fountain Of Knowledge

I hadn't seen a human since starting the trip, but coming down the trail was a white haired, white bearded old gentleman who looked to be in fantastic shape for his age. We stopped and chatted a few minutes and I discovered that he was a local, who knew the area like the back of his hand. I mentioned my dilemma of not knowing the trail and that my maps only covered the area to the West but that I wanted to see the most interesting and beautiful places in the mountains. His eyes lit up as he thought a few seconds and asked me how many days I planned to hike. I told him I could stay a maximum of 9 more days and he paused, deep in thought and calculation. Soon he started thinking out loud, changing his opinion a couple of times as his memory came up with better ideas. Finally he told me he had the best trip, the one he would do if it were his first or only time in the area. This hike would take me to the North and East, meaning I would have no maps to fall back on in case of emergency. This "Fountain Of Knowledge" took a 3 by 5 index card and a pen out of his shirt pocket, wrote down the directions on one side and a simple, crude map on the other side and handed it to me to make sure I wouldn't forget and get lost. He then explained it to me, pointing toward the area I would be hiking. I asked a few questions which he politely and knowledgeably answered. He then quizzed me until he was sure I understood each change of trail then hurried off on his way. I stood a few minutes going over his directions and wished I could have spoken with him for hours. The things I could have learned from this kind old sage, but he still had miles to go before dark and was smart enough not to let me delay him too long.

CHAPTER SIX

On Top Of The World

A couple hours later I was feeling excited, when I reached the Ranger Fire Tower, but was exhausted, and breathing hard due to the elevation, and the steep strenuous trail while carrying a nearly full 70 pound pack. It was the highest point of the area and in every direction for miles I was looking down on forests, meadows, hills, mountain peaks, valleys, clouds, cliffs, and trees, with not a road in sight. This was truly wilderness. It was a feast for my eyes and peace for my soul. I dropped my pack and spent nearly an hour walking around and soaking up the breathtaking view. It was no wonder the Fire Tower was located here. A ranger with binoculars in the tower could probably see smoke a hundred miles away if a fire broke out. It was late afternoon, and I was glad the trail headed downhill. The trail toward White Creek followed a ridge that opened into the biggest, most beautiful, alpine meadow I had ever seen.   From a distance, the meadow resembled a sea of tall green grass with occasional islands of trees rising from its depths. Scattered throughout the scene were areas of colorful flowers. It was the most inviting scene imaginable. Someone watching from a distance might have thought I was drunk, disoriented or confused because every few steps I would look to the right to take in the view then turn around, and walk backwards a few steps to see the view behind me. Then I would look to my right again to view the scenery in the opposite direction, then turn around to walk forward again constantly moving toward the meadow. Occasionally I would stop and drink in the stunning beauty hoping to memorize it for future enjoyment when back home. Toward the far end of the meadow was a weathered old wooden forest service sign indicating the presence of a spring only a few hundred yards off trail. I walked over to the spring which was in a forested area, took off my pack and sat down to rest and refill my canteens. While enjoying the task at hand, the words of the Psalm came back to me forcefully, powerfully and personally. "The Lord is my shepherd, I shall not want. He makes me lie down in green pastures, He leads me beside still waters." Here I was, relaxing near this beautiful green meadow while drinking and filling my canteens from "the still waters" of this mountain spring. I felt as though I was reliving King David's experience! I was alone in the midst of a most peaceful and beautiful setting imaginable and I was being watched over and taken care of by an unseen, unbelievably compassionate Being. "He restores my soul, He leads me in the paths of righteousness for His name's sake." It was a moving moment. My spirit was being refreshed and revitalized. I was never more alone than in this majestic, magnificent wilderness, hours from the nearest human, days from civilization by foot, yet I felt closer than ever to my Shepherd. He was greater and closer than the bears, mountain lions and other wildlife I knew were nearby, only unobservable by my physical five senses. Unlike David, my experience with a shepherd was non-existent and my knowledge of sheep was extremely limited, but the words written so long ago had deep meaning and brought great comfort. The moment was rich and would be relived many times, but my canteens and soul were full and it was time to be on my way.

CHAPTER SEVEN

Holy Night

Camp this night was on a ridge with a fabulous view of the sky unencumbered by trees. The last several nights had been cloudy with intermittent rain, but this night was so clear I decided to sleep under the stars. With no city lights or distractions for dozens of miles and a thinner atmosphere due to the 10,000' elevation, the star filled sky was startling. As far as the eye could see were tiny lights, bright to dim, large to small, white to bluish to red, some alone, others in clusters. The Milky Way covered the middle of the sky like milk spilled across a painting. Every few minutes a light blazed across the darkness, sometimes only a flash, but other times seemingly never-ending. The sky was so dark and clear that some lights moved silently above from one end of the sky to the other. I knew these to be satellites or possibly even the space station. Nights like this never failed to humble me in awe of the grandeur and power and artistry of the Creator of all that I could see.

At times, just for brief moments, I felt almost trapped on this tiny orb called earth as I viewed the enormous, unending palette spread overhead. Sometimes perspective is everything. While walking in this mountain wilderness

I felt like a tiny, insignificant speck. The 10 to 15 miles I had hiked had taken all day and I was exhausted when I stopped for the night. From my perspective the earth was limitless. To explore only the major mountainous areas of the world at my piddling pace would consume several lifetimes. The earth from this perspective was huge beyond comprehension. Yet, as I looked up into the vast expanse above, the earth suddenly seemed tiny and insignificant. One star, the red one in the constellation Orion's left shoulder called Betelgeuse, if placed next to our sun would make the sun appear the size of a pea in comparison. If Betelgeuse were located at our sun, all four of the inner planets would orbit inside this flaming behemoth. Of course in reality this burning furnace of atomic energy would instantly consume Mercury, Venus, Earth, and Mars. Yet Betelgeuse was simply a bright reddish dot in the night sky from my perspective. I drifted into an imaginary journey traveling to Mars and exploring our solar system's largest volcano, 15-mile high, Olympus Mons. I saw the Great Red Spot of Jupiter from its surface after flying through it from above, then explored Jupiter's icy moon Europa and found the elusive liquid water deep inside. How incredible it was to fly close to Saturn and view the unique ring system from every angle, then to observe a pulsar and binary star system up close but from a safe distance. I dreamed of exploring another solar system to see what mysteries its planets would reveal and what theories would need to be re-examined and refined to answer all the questions the unexpected discoveries would reveal. I became mentally exhausted trying unsuccessfully to imagine the billions of suns in the billions of galaxies and the many enigmas astronomers have discovered without answers.

A commercial jet passed high overhead unheard but easily seen and my mind switched gears to the mundane and absurd. Where was the plane heading and from where had it come? How many passengers were onboard? Had they already been served a meal? Were they watching a movie or reading or sleeping? How nice it would have been if a flight attendant could have dropped a six-pack of ice cold beverages attached to a parachute for me to find. I fell asleep back in the mountain wilderness far from home and civilization but much, much closer than I had just been.

CHAPTER EIGHT

Pain And Laughter

After nearly an hour hiking down a steep, rugged, rocky trail through a narrow canyon mid-morning the next day, my feet and knees were in pain. Hiking up steep trails with a full pack is difficult. It causes profuse sweating, makes the lungs scream for air and the muscles burn, but can be done at a slow pace with frequent pauses to catch your breath and rest the muscles. Going down a steep hill, especially one with jagged rocks, is an entirely different proposition. The slower you go the more your muscles and knees ache. The faster you go the more your feet are pummeled by the sharp rocks as the combined weight of pack and body pounds into the ground. Slow or fast, pick your torture. To ease the pain I drifted into the spiritual world, thinking again of the 23rd Psalm. "The Lord is my Shepherd, I shall not want." What exactly did that statement or promise "I shall not want" mean? I WANTED. In fact I WANTED plenty. I WANTED an escalator, or better yet the "It" (now called Segway) that had just been invented and revealed with great fanfare. A gyroscopic, motorized two wheeled scooter of some kind that was supposed to revolutionize transportation, as we know it. "It" wouldn't last long out here I was certain. So okay, I WANTED a horse. Let the horse take the beating. They are powerfully built for travel and could easily carry me AND my pack. As long as I was WANTING, I WANTED a shower and a milkshake and a greasy hamburger. But wait a minute. One of the reasons I was here was to push myself to the limit. To make sure I was still somewhat tough and hadn't gotten too soft and mushy in my old age from all the modern conveniences. When I left I WANTED to get away (at least for a while) from the things I was now WANTING. Okay, so "I shall not want" probably more accurately meant I wouldn't need, or at least my life wouldn't be in danger from not having something I really needed to keep me alive. What kind of life would it be if I never had an unfulfilled WANT?

I was abruptly brought back to reality when, rounding a corner, I startled a wild turkey up the hill and ahead to my right. It ran downhill several feet in front of me, leapt into the air flapping its wings and was instantly airborne. It then turned, flew up the canyon in the direction I was heading and was soon out of sight. It was an interesting and humorous sight. That big fat turkey was actually flying above the trees, yet it was the noisiest, heaviest and least graceful flying creature I had ever seen. I laughed every time I replayed that sight in my mind.

Majestic Magnificent Powerfully Frightening STORM

I noticed the sky becoming dark and foreboding when I saw a flash of light in the distance. Seconds later, as I set my pack down to get out the poncho, I heard the rumble of not-too-distant thunder. By the time I had my pack covered and was putting on the poncho, a gust of rain-filled wind hit. This storm was going to be ferocious. I pulled the tarp, which was normally only used for protection at night, off the pack, found a relatively level place close by next to a tree, to sit down and pulled the tarp over and under me for added protection. I wasn't extremely worried about lightning, being in a steep canyon with numerous tall trees around. Now that I was under the tarp, the wind and rain seemed far less of a threat. I sat patiently and relaxed, watching with interest as the powerful storm engulfed the area.

Back in civilization, TV, a book, or a computer were the entertainment of choice. Here the entertainment wasn't of my choosing, but was far more exciting and all encompassing. The entertainment being provided free of charge for me involved all five of my senses, not merely the two it would take back home. The sky disappeared entirely as heavy blackness filled the canyon.

Wind howled through the trees and bushes and over the rocks and cliffs. I

clung to the tarp and backpack keeping them from falling over or blown away

by the fierce force. The flashes of light interrupted the darkness and the

booming, roaring sound of the thunder increased in intensity and frequency. A

nearby flash erupted so bright it stung my eyes. An instant later the ground

under and all around me shook. A powerful, frightening crash and deep

rumbling roar swept through the valley for what seemed like minutes. Before

the rumbling stopped there was a simultaneous ear shattering explosion and

flash that felt as if it lifted me off the ground and dropped me. Instantly all I

could see was blue. My eyelids had never closed and I didn't see a blindingly

bright flash like before, but now every direction I turned all I saw was

blue...not trees...not ground...not rain...just blue! I smelled, felt and even

tasted electricity. I wondered if this was what it was like to be blind and for a

moment, I panicked. How would I find my way out of here if I couldn't see?

How would I make camp at night and how would I load all my necessities on my

pack in the morning? If I found my way back to the car, how would I drive

home? My cell phone didn't get a signal in the area so it was worthless.

Another terrifying blast rattled the trees, the rocks, even me. But now I could

see again! The blue was gone and I could see the trees and rain. I was

relieved, but the peacefulness of this place was shattered along with my

confidence. The power displayed was beyond comprehension. The blinding

arching light and teeth rattling thunder were simply evidence of awesome and deadly forces. I felt alone, as if my life was of no consequence, in this dark

foreboding valley. I was being pummeled by rain, hail and wind and

bombarded by noises so loud and so close, they frightened me to the very core.

I was scared, but knowing the Author of this terrifying masterpiece, I prayed

for His protection. Rain whipped every direction, pounding powerfully against

the tarp, the trees, the rocks and the creek. The combination of wind, rain

and lightning cleansed as it washed through the vegetation, removing the

weak, the old and the very young. As my eyes and ears became accustomed to

the brilliant flashes and noisy crashes, different sounds, emanating from many

directions raised concern. It took several minutes for me to realize that the

storm was dislodging loose rocks from above, sending them rolling and

bouncing down the hillside into the valley. My ears told me that some were

landing dangerously close. I stood, rain pelting my face as I surveyed the

situation to determine the safest course of action. Thirty feet below was the

creek that cut through this canyon. Looking closer, I was surprised to see that

the water level had risen over a foot in the short time since the storm began.

If the rain continued for hours, a wall of water could stampede through the

canyon wreaking destruction in the flash flood's path. Moving lower was not an

option. Not far away there were two large sturdy trees that I was sure had

stood for many years on the other side of this relatively level area. I decided it

would be much safer and even more comfortable to lean against one of those

huge trees. I slipped twice moving only sixty feet while carrying my pack in front of me and struggling with the tarp. Walking over slippery rocks and vegetation off trail was dangerous, but sitting on the downhill side of the tree should protect me from any falling rocks. As the poet Joyce Kilmer once said, "only God can make a tree" and now I found a new use for these magnificent peaceful giants.

The storm droned on and on. Occasionally the rain would be joined by pea sized hail and even through the poncho and tarp I felt the sting. For an hour and a half I watched, heard, smelled, felt, tasted and enjoyed the excitement taking place all around, with only mild apprehension now. As time passed my mind evaluated the options. If the storm lasted much longer I would have to make camp somewhere nearby while trying to stay dry and comfortable. I would probably forego the difficulty of cooking a meal under the circumstances and settle for anything simple and easy. Dinner would probably consist of water from my canteen, a granola bar and a container of pudding. The real chore would be getting comfortable enough to sleep while keeping everything dry. It would be pretty difficult to set up the tent and keep everything dry with rain this heavy. If the storm continued until dark, I already knew from the short move to the tree, that hiking to a better location was out of the question.

This wasn't home. At home my wife and I would fix a delicious hot dinner from the safety of our kitchen, enjoy it from the convenience of the kitchen table, after which we would sit in the comfort of our living room and read, watch TV, talk or listen to music. Upon retiring to the peacefulness of the bedroom I would use the bathroom with all its numerous amenities then fall asleep lying in the plush, soft, roomy bed, dry warm, and comfortable. At home I would probably even forget there was a storm. Tonight, if the storm continued, my hope was that I could get by without nature calling. There are few tasks less pleasant than digging a hole in the mud during pouring rain and using "the facility" while struggling to keep yourself, your clothing and the paper dry.

The words came back once more. This time the following verse grabbed my attention. "Yea though I walk through the valley of the shadow of death, I will fear no evil. For you are with me. Your rod and your staff they comfort me." I was amazed! Again I felt as though I was reliving David's Psalm. I was walking through the valley of the shadow of death. On one side was the danger of a flash flood, while on the other, rocks were tumbling all around. David's statement was comforting beyond measure. "I will fear no evil, for you are with me, your rod and your staff they comfort me." A rod sounded like a weapon where a staff sounded more like a tool or a walking stick to me. But no matter, David didn't fear and his Shepherd was also my Shepherd. The tree was shielding me from the falling rocks and though I was damp I certainly wasn't soaked. I was even able to rest sitting back leaning against the tree. As a matter of fact, my feet and legs were no longer hurting! I spent a long time thanking and praising my unseen Shepherd who was looking over me in spite of the difficult yet exciting situation. The storm passed, the darkness became

light, the rain stopped and the birds and other animals came out to play, eat

and chatter.

CHAPTER TEN

Scat Entertainment

It's funny when alone for days on end what you find to amuse or entertain yourself. I had taken to examining animal tracks and scat. It wasn't difficult to identify several types of tracks and dung. I have often seen dog, cat, raccoon and deer tracks and droppings. I knew that coyote, fox and wolf were similar enough to dog to be roughly identified. It surprised me how much could be determined from examining animal dung in detail. When trying to understand what type of animals were near, dung was always available even if tracks weren't. This wasn't an art I practiced often back home. But out here, there was so much, of so many different varieties available for study that it was fascinating to know which animals and in what quantity were nearby. I discovered that deer droppings were very common, simple small roundish pellets. Elk droppings were similar but larger and normally more moist. Fox dung was shaped a lot like small dog droppings but with twists and usually had some berry or seed remains in them. As I became more familiar with dung it became fairly easy to tell if it was fresh or old. Obviously, the more odor the fresher it was, while the dryer the older it was. Coyote and wolf were similar while bear was in a class all its own. I saw bear dung regularly, even very fresh droppings, though I never once saw a bear. The same was true of mountain

lions and bobcats. Their dung was occasionally evident and tracks could be

seen rarely but the elusive nocturnal creatures remained hidden.

At times I would spend several minutes breaking dung apart to see what

the animal had eaten. It became quite an interesting game to guess what kind

of animal it was from, how big it was and how long ago it had made its deposit.

Once I spotted a relatively large deposit that had an almost hairlike covering.

As I broke into it with a stick, I noticed what looked like a small oyster or

clamshell inside. Upon further examination I discovered two such "shell pairs"

and I wondered how this creature, which I assumed to be a cat of some sort,

had gotten a clam or oyster in the mountains. The mountain oysters I had

heard about certainly didn't have shells. This detective type work made my

new found hobby interesting so I probed further. I separated the "shells"

completely from the dung and cleaned them enough with the stick and some

leaves only to discover to my amazement that they weren't shells at all. What

I had at first thought were shells turned out to be the beaks of fairly good-sized

birds. The cat that had deposited this dung was fast enough to have caught

two birds in one attack. No future discoveries came close to the intrigue of

this unusual specimen.

<u>CHAPTER ELEVEN</u>

Better Than Popcorn And A Movie

The bearded old man had directed me well when he sent me to White Creek. When I first met up with the creek it was very plain and ordinary and a bit of a disappointment. The creek flowed through a wide open valley and was surrounded by shrubs and trees. In places it was marshy, probably due to all the rain that had saturated the area. At first I tromped in and out of the water and mud following the creek trail. After a while, the creek became deeper and flowed more swiftly and the trail became rocky and dry. The valley grew more picturesque with steep high cliffs on both sides. The trail crossed White Creek and directly ahead in the middle of the level grass covered field was a huge, beautiful probably 100 year old log cabin with a 50' tall, perfectly symmetrical blue spruce directly in front. Mountain cliffs rose abruptly on two sides of the field with White Creek flowing beside the log cabin. This was a picture perfect post-card scene.

I laid my pack down by the cabin and explored the surrounding area. A short distance behind the cabin was a shallow pond that (I learned later) had many years previous been used as a fish hatchery to stock the mountain creeks with rainbow and brown trout. Off to one side was a trail leading up a hill toward a cliff. Hidden out of sight was a sturdy old two-hole outhouse! The

area on both sides of the trail and surrounding the outhouse was loaded with

raspberry plants that were filled with perfectly ripe fruit. I spent a long time

enjoying nature's bounty. The fruit was irresistibly sweet and delicious after

days of eating oatmeal and granola bars. I picked and ate and enjoyed

succulent fruit, fresher than any found in a grocery store. The price was

certainly right also. I admired and appreciated the folks who had, many years

earlier, put their effort into cultivating this enormous patch of wild treats.

Had I not stopped to explore, I would have passed by the area and missed the

feast I was enjoying. After my banquet, it was time to use the long neglected,

but practically palatial, two-hole facility. While sitting and listening to the

peaceful sound of the creek and the breeze the words of the psalm popped

back into my head. "You prepare a table before me in the presence of my

enemies. You anoint my head with oil. My cup runs over. Surely goodness and

mercy will follow me all the days of my life, and I will dwell in the house of the

Lord forever." I may not have had a literal table out here, but the delicious

meal I just experienced couldn't have tasted any better on a table made of

gold, nor on a Rockefeller or king's table. In fact, the beauty of my

surroundings beat any table I had ever eaten on. I didn't know who or where

my enemies might be out here, but if there were any they were out of sight

and out of mind and God had kept them away so far. Shortly before stopping

here, I had bent down and dipped my hot and dusty head in the creek, washing the dirt off my face and head and refreshing my soul. My cup certainly was

running over. I had all the water I could use, it was ice cold and thirst

quenching, and spread out before me were more raspberries than I could eat in

a week. I felt as though goodness and mercy were definitely following me.

Right now not one immediate want was left unfulfilled. The trials,

frustrations, pressure and temptations of normal everyday life existed for the

moment in that other far away world. Everywhere I looked was beauty and

peace. If this was the house of the Lord, and how could it not be, I wanted to

experience it, live it, enjoy it all the days of my life and forever.

Being here, surrounded by simplicity and beauty was a stark contrast to

the excesses and constant bombardment of almost continuous temptations

experienced daily in modern society. We have comforts beyond comprehension

mostly taken for granted. We have more to eat, and drink and to consume our

time with, than a lifetime would allow. Yet for all the time savers and

conveniences we have created, we rarely make time to experience and enjoy

the truly important things life has to offer. I felt as though I might just be the

most blessed man on earth at this moment. To be in this place enjoying its

beauty and tranquility, while having an intimate and special relationship with

the Being who had created it all, was precious and amazingly delightful. I had

heard people tell me that God had spoken to them and I was jealous. He had

never talked to me. As much as I wished He would, He had never told me

which direction to go with my life or which decision would bring the best results. Yet here I was in His backyard and at every turn He was putting David's most meaningful words into my mind. I was experiencing, in a very different time and in a very different way, some of what the ancient King of Israel had experienced and felt and written about several thousand years before. Could this be His way of communicating with me? Was He letting me know that in spite of His silence in my life (or was it my deafness) nonetheless I was very special to Him?

Exploring the area around the old hatchery, the interesting log cabin and beautiful spruce took well into the late afternoon. Following White Creek downstream the canyon narrowed until rock walls rose straight up on both sides. The creek flowed through the rock canyon with water settling in deep clear pools, then flowing out forming breathtaking cascades and waterfalls. Inside this canyon it was possible to stand on the cliffs, overlooking the deep pools and jump or dive distances of 20 to 30 feet or more into the clear cold deep water, never touching bottom.

I jumped into the cold water, and swam in the deep pools, exploring their secrets. Bathing under the waterfalls, washing a week's accumulation of dirt, sweat and odor from my body was pure ecstasy. I played in the frigid water until I was shivering, then climbed onto, and laid on, the sun warmed rocks, to dry off and soak up the warmth. Within minutes the sound of the water and warmth put me to sleep, until a noise or pesky bug woke me and I moved to another of the many pools for an encore..

The refreshing, exciting, stimulating experience entertained me for several hours. It was a clean, completely exhausted yet thoroughly refreshed and rejuvenated, happy backpacker who made his way back to the meadow with the cabin shortly before dark.

CHAPTER TWELVE

Intruders

I set up camp on the opposite side of White Creek from the cabin. It was on slightly higher ground in a small level meadow with trees spread throughout. While eating dinner a loud noise from across the creek startled me. I sat bolt upright listening and watching in the direction from which the sound had just come. Soon I heard what sounded like several very large animals or people jumping in the hatchery pond behind the cabin. Trees blocked my view of the pond but I was glad I had explored the whole area in case I had to make a quick get away. I heard more splashing sounds but no voices or laughing so I assumed large animals were enjoying the water. Could it be bears? If so, I wanted to stay alert and ready to move if necessary. It wasn't long before the creatures came out of the water and the sounds were moving directly toward me. The time slowed to a glacier like pace as I anticipated and wondered what might be moving towards me. The sounds slowly grew louder and closer as the animals seemed in no hurry. Finally they appeared. In front of me stood three large beautiful elk cows and one bull. Though I sat motionless and silent they seemed startled to see me. They stood quietly and watched for a long time. Then one made a sound like the noise a person with no musical experience blowing on a trumpet might make. I had heard this sound at night many times and always wondered what animal it came from. Now I knew first hand and up close. The majestic creatures slowly moved away into the dark, occasionally bellowing for my benefit. This night I slept soundly and peacefully, with the benefit of being clean and totally exhausted.

CHAPTER THIRTEEN

Spider Lessons And Tree Questions

From the time I left White Creek I was heading back in the direction of my vehicle, which meant I was heading toward home. Though I was still at least four days away from the car, I was struck by the realization that this trip was more than half over. I looked forward to being home and seeing my family and friends, but I also knew I would miss this wilderness, its rugged beauty and the special bond that had developed on this trip with my lone Companion and Confidant. The morning while hiking up out of White Creek canyon, I knew I would someday return to this very beautiful and special place. Whether another solo trip or one with friends or family I didn't know, but God willing I would be back.

Arising early one morning to the call of nature, I immediately became entangled in the sticky, irritating fine threads of a large spider's nightlong masterpiece. Walking toward my destination, arms flailing to remove the maddening substance, every few steps I encountered more spiders' webs until I stopped, yelled in frustration, and wiped wildly with my hands to remove the aggravating threads. I spit to get the silky sticky stuff out of my mouth and yelled at the architects of evil. If it was possible to hate a tiny creature for simply gathering breakfast, at that moment I was guilty. I'm sure if the little things had minds, they would have hated me more for destroying their night's work and depriving them of their next meal. Later on, several times during the day I relived the creepy feeling of sticky web strings in my hair, on my face and ears and arms. Each time I imagined a huge eight-legged thing running around on my head or inside my shirt making more ooey, gooey spitooeys and leaving them all over my body. I shuddered at the thought and the morning's memory.

During the day's journey I hiked through an open level area with only a small scattering of trees. The area contained many extremely tall ponderosa pines spread out over the area giving it an open uncluttered look. While walking and thinking I heard a thunderous boom and felt the ground shake. Since there were no storm clouds in the sky, my first thought was that it could be an earthquake. Then the idea of a boulder falling off a cliff entered my mind, but there were no cliffs within sight. I put my pack down and walked in the direction the sound had come from. Being alone with no pressing schedule I enjoyed investigating the mysterious things beyond my experience. It was fun being a detective and trying to figure out the cause of things that weren't obviously apparent. Many things could make a noise out here but the boulder theory was eliminated right away. The sky was mostly clear, so even if there had been freak lightening it would never have made the ground shake. Another idea that didn't stand up to the test of examination. As I neared the edge of the alpine meadow I noticed a huge Ponderosa Pine laying flat on the ground. I walked over to its base and found a dirt clump where its roots were and a large

hole where the dirt clump covered roots had been. This more than 100 year-

old tree had apparently just fallen over as I was walking nearby! I had noticed

trees in this condition during my trip, but this was the first one I had ever been

close to at the very moment it fell. I remembered now that the other trees I

had seen in this condition had holes mostly filled with water from all the rain.

This hole was practically empty and mostly dry. All the data seemed to indicate

that I had found the cause of the noise and shaking. I couldn't help but smile

as I remembered the time worn question, "If a tree falls in the forest and no

one is there to hear it did it make a sound?" I always thought the question was

stupid. So I came up with a few stupid questions of my own. What are the

odds of someone being there when the tree in the forest actually falls? What if

a deaf person was walking under the tree when it fell and it fell on them and

killed them? Since no one heard the tree fall would the deaf person still be

dead? What if the dead person wasn't deaf? Would they have felt the tree as

it fell and killed them? Would they have known what hit them? Would the tree

that killed the person have made a sound if it fell on them and killed them

before it hit the ground? Am I coming up with such goofy questions because

I've been out in the wilderness all alone with no one to talk to, too long? Could

anyone come up with a question that makes sense with so many "to's" in the

last five words of the sentence? I knew it was time to move on and change

gears, and fast.

My camp this night was under a few trees near a babbling brook. After dinner I hiked up a hill to have a look at the surrounding terrain. My camp was in a valley with a brook flowing through. Small hills were on the north and south sides with the meadow in the middle and the brook carving its way from east to west. The view of the quiet valley was lovely from my vantage point high above. It was an awesome place to spend time thanking the Creator of this view, for a safe trip, for sight that allowed me to appreciate the view, and for so many other things often taken for granted.

When I finally made it back down to camp I was ready to hit the sack. It was a warm, somewhat humid, windless night. I lay on top of my sleeping bag, as was my custom on warm nights. The moon was waning but still nearly full, providing plenty of light as I started to drift off to sleep. Just then I heard that annoying buzzing sound. This was the first night that mosquitoes were a problem. I got up, found the Off in my pack and sprayed generous portions on all my exposed skin and hair. I didn't like the smell or the stickiness, but mosquitoes have to be the worst pests in the entire outdoors. A bite on a knuckle or an elbow is painful to scratch. Anywhere else the itching is simply an irritation but certainly no fun. The worst part is unquestionably the high pitched buzz as the ugly creature darts from ear to ear searching for a juicy place to land. I lay back down hoping the repellent would live up to its name. These mosquitoes were apparently hungry and persistent. They would fly around my head for minutes trying unsuccessfully to find a repellent-free landing zone. I wasn't being bitten, but the incessant high-pitched buzzing was

torture. I began swatting to drive them away but it was to no long-term avail.

For a while I lay perfectly still on my back on top of the sleeping bag and

looked up at the sky trying to ignore their whining attacks. In the corner of my

eye I noticed movement and something glistening very close by. I turned and

looked closer only to discover a spider building its web between a couple trees

not far above my head. To my surprise the web already had several mosquitoes

stuck in it! Over the next minutes I watched the spider moving rapidly up and

down, back and forth with the sticky silk thread trailing from its rear. While I

watched, she finished the web and made a quick snack of the pesky

mosquitoes. I found myself cheering for the spider, encouraging her as another

mosquito became trapped in her intricate work of art. In no time this amazing

creature accomplished what my repellent couldn't. The mosquitoes were no

longer bothering me and my hero was the creature whose sisters I had

assaulted and tried to destroy only a dozen hours ago. I repented of my

formerly evil ways and thoughts. I praised this spider and told her she had

nothing to worry about from me. I have never been so glad to see a creature I

had been so unhappy with earlier in the day. This evening I learned a lesson of

nature that I wouldn't soon forget.

When I awoke rather late the next morning, I lay lazily thinking and

watching the sky as the sun began peeking through the valley. I looked toward

it and saw a beautiful masterpiece as exquisite as any stained glass window I had ever seen, formed by moisture clinging to the spider's web and the sun's light shining on the web. The light refracted through sections of the dew laden web with a bright variety of colors and light reflections, sparkling and bursting from it, creating an amazing masterpiece of colorful art. My appreciation of spiders had grown enormously in the last twentyfour hours!

CHAPTER FOURTEEN

A Lost Art Recovered

Near mid-day while enjoying a snack I heard voices and noises up ahead. I was cautiously excited, not having seen a human for several days now, so I picked up the pace a bit. Within minutes three people on horseback came into view. I started to greet them only to squawk something unintelligible. I immediately realized I hadn't spoken aloud for four days. After swallowing some water and attempting to speak again my voice recovered. We began parrying to discover who each other was and what the other was doing out here. The three were a local rancher, his wife and one of their ranch-hands on an excursion to scout the area for bull elk. The season would begin in a few weeks and they wanted to be prepared. They asked if I had seen any elk or signs of them and where. I asked numerous questions about the cabin and pond and was delighted to find that one of the rancher's relatives had built the cabin and he related some interesting history of the area to me. They may have thought it strange when I questioned them about wolf and bear dung, but they confirmed my conclusions. They asked if I had seen many bear and were surprised to hear that I hadn't seen any. When I explained that I had seen a lot of bear dung they told me bears were plentiful all around the area. I was amazed when they said they hadn't seen any but knew they were near because their horses spooked whenever one was close or had recently been close by. Before parting I showed the ranchers my new GPS. They were enthralled and said they would buy one before elk season started. After parting ways, I replayed our conversation enjoying the new information gleaned from them.

Shortly before dusk, after a long day of hiking, I was finally out of the valley and could see Iron Creek Lake. It would be getting dark soon so I didn't waste time exploring around the lake since it was a small and obviously shallow lake. I decided to keep going without filling my canteens after seeing the green algae covered water.

CHAPTER FIFTEEN

Dinner To Die For

Just up trail from the lake I set up camp for what would be my next to last night in the wilderness. My dinner choice was easy compared to the first night when my pack held meals for a dozen days. My wife had contributed a few low-calorie, freeze dried meals in boxes she had purchased. They were very light-weight and, being a practical person, I decided to save them until last, eating the heavier meals first. This particular one was a hamburger with bun and meat sealed in separate plastic pouches. The instructions were to boil the pouch with the meat for five minutes then remove and place between the bun. Simple enough. Upon completion of boiling I searched my pack unsuccessfully for condiments. Dry meat was placed on dry bun absent any smell. Big bite followed by chewing absent any taste. I searched the pack again for anything to enhance the dining experience. Nothing. I had used the boiled water to make hot chocolate so I tried dipping the "hamburger" into the hot chocolate to make it palatable. The combination of hunger and chocolate flavor did the trick. I'll never know, but it's possible that dipping the box in hot chocolate might have made it edible too. I ate both boxes of hamburgers which the packaging claimed was a total of 250 calories. My wife later informed me that both she and her daughter had tried unsuccessfully to choke down those hamburgers while dieting. One bite had them gagging (even with condiments) and the remains hit the trash. She was too frugal to throw out the last two packages, hence I inherited them. One of her first questions when I returned home was how did I like the hamburger, thinking my reaction would match hers. She couldn't believe I had actually finished both especially with nothing on them.

CHAPTER SIXTEEN

Deadly Decision

After dinner I laid out the items I would need for breakfast and repacked the backpack. It bothered me that I had neglected to fill the canteens before leaving the creek, but I had assumed the lake would provide good drinking water. After using water for breakfast in the morning I would be left with only one full and one half full canteen. Water had never been a problem on this trip and it was only seven and a half miles to the spring just past Hummingbird Saddle. For all I knew there would be springs and creeks along the trail but I still hated not heeding my own advice to never leave a water source without full canteens. My camp was at 8,000' elevation and tomorrow I would be going to Hummingbird Saddle, which was just below 11,000'. A good night's sleep was a necessity because tomorrow was going to be one tough haul up a mighty steep trail.

I started the morning at a steady pace after a breakfast of oatmeal and raisins. Muscles and joints, once warmed up, always felt great in the morning after eight or ten hours sleep. The old body's initial stiffness from a night sleeping on hard cold ground gave way quickly to the exercise of the hike. The trail began with a gentle uphill slope. Knowing the elevation gain ahead I was mildly surprised. It became evident quickly that this trail was seldom used and

not maintained. In places the trail was difficult to see, making it difficult to

follow. At other times fallen trees forced backtracking or long side trips from

which it was often hard to find the trail again. There were several instances

when I had to stop because the trail had disappeared. I studied the area

closely but, not able to see a trail in any direction, I was forced to backtrack to

the last place it was visible. I would then spend considerable time searching

the area until I found the trail's direction again. It was a challenge I somewhat

enjoyed, in spite of the extra time and distance it added to the day's hike.

By mid-day the trail was still fairly level. It was a steady (with the

exception of all the detours to find the lost trail) but easy uphill slope. I

wondered numerous times how much elevation I had gained. My Garmin GPS

was a lifesaver most of the time, but this trail was so overgrown with trees that

I had difficulty receiving clear satellite signals long enough to get elevation

readings. It was a fairly warm day and cloud cover was nonexistent. By the

time I stopped for lunch, in spite of rationing, I had finished the half canteen

and part of the full one. Granola bars weren't great thirst quenchers, so by

the time I started out again after lunch, I was down to just over half a canteen

of water. My hope was that, in spite of the difficulty following the trail and all

the backtracking I had done, I was at least four miles up trail. If I was, then

only about three and a half miles remained to the spring at Hummingbird

Saddle. This trail hadn't yielded a spring, a creek, or even a drop of water so far. Oh well, at least I knew there was water ahead even if the distance to it remained a mystery. The real question was why hadn't this trail become steeper. To go from 8,000' to 11,000' elevation the trail should be one tough bunch of steep switchbacks, yet it wasn't. Whatever mysteries or surprises lay ahead, they would soon be revealed.

I was glad that I had saved a bunch of Werther's hard caramel candies. There's nothing like sucking on a Werther's to keep the saliva flowing and a moist mouth when water is scarce. Shortly after lunch the terrain changed. Usually when a trail becomes extremely steep, it begins to switch back and forth along the hillside. I've often thought it would be better to find a trail that went straight up the hill, that skipped the back and forth and saved the extra steps even at the expense of being steeper and more difficult to climb. The tough part would be over sooner that way wouldn't it? I was about to get a lesson in life, even though I've hiked thousands of miles of mountain trails in my thirty plus years of backpacking.

Now I could tell why this trail was so neglected. Nobody in his or her right mind would have chosen to hike this trail going uphill. The trail was ascending at nearly a thirty-degree angle as far as I could see. Soon I was leaning forward and my pace slowed dramatically. Even with the far slower pace I was sucking air as if I were running the gun lap of a mile race. It was impossible to get the air my body craved breathing through my nose, so my mouth became as dry as sandpaper. The cotton mouth caused coughing and occasional gagging. I was popping the Werther's into my mouth at an alarming rate to alleviate the problem. My heart was pumping so hard it felt like a hammer in my chest. I kept the slow steady pace for what seemed like an hour, but might have been much less.

My philosophy when hiking to get to a specific destination, was to set whatever pace was comfortable and then not stop unless there was some overwhelming reason. Simply taking a break wasn't a good enough reason. I rarely deviated from that plan, but now I was forced to stop so my body could cool down. Sweat was pouring from my forehead and all over the rest of my body. My shirt, and to a lesser degree my shorts, were soaked. I stopped and found a tree to lean against so I could rest without sitting down. It took several minutes before my heartbeat fell back to a quieter, more normal pace and I could once again breathe with my mouth closed. I took a sip of water from the last canteen and swished it around in my mouth for a long time before swallowing the precious liquid. My canteen held only two or three more swallows. At the rate I was sweating I would become dehydrated in no time. Prior to dehydration I would start coughing and gagging from cottonmouth and dry throat. For the first time on this fabulous trip my situation appeared desperate. As I stood relaxing and catching my breath I noticed, in stark contrast to my difficulty, the beauty of the flowers and vegetation in this area. I was standing at the edge of a sunflower patch. Hummingbirds and bees and butterflies and moths, and I was sure dozens of unseen critters, were enjoying the bounty of the area.

"Yea though I walk through the valley of the shadow of death I will fear no evil, for you are with me. Your rod and your staff they comfort me." I humbly called out to Him. "I know You're here with me. I know You realize that if I have a heart attack out here so far from hospitals and civilization it's all over for me in this life. I know You understand the struggle I'm having and how much water I need and how far it is to the next water source. I know You've been with me the last ten days of this trip and have protected me from a terrible storm and lightening and blindness and probably dozens of other dangers I wasn't even aware of. I ask for your continued protection and guidance the rest of my journey. I pray that you would provide the water I need before my body becomes too dehydrated to function properly. This trip has brought me closer to You and taught me so much about You and about myself and Your awesome creation. I hope you will allow me to live life and pass on to others some of what I've learned."

I pushed off from the tree I was leaning against and continued up the steep slope. I felt much better after the five or ten minutes rest, but in only thirty or forty steps my heart was pounding and I was huffing and puffing. My pace was painfully slow and keeping even this pace without stopping was difficult. One step, a few seconds rest, then another step was the best I was able to do up this inhumanely steep slope. I was sucking air like a vacuum cleaner and all my hard candies were gone. I tried controlling my breathing in order to keep my mouth shut but to no avail. If I kept my mouth closed I would wasn't getting enough air, yet keeping it open to breathe was causing dry mouth so bad I coughed regularly. It was twenty minutes at least that I had been moving. Stopping again was a necessity even though it went against every instinct. I looked back and realized I had covered quite a distance and was much higher than before. It was a boost for my sagging morale until I looked ahead to find there was no let up in sight.

This time I took off my pack and lay flat on my back to rest. I opened one canteen and
 held it up to let the last drops drain into my parched mouth. It was now mid Saturday afternoon. As I lay resting, I decided that no matter what happened I had to keep going until I came to the spring and could get water even if it meant hiking late into the night in the dark. As dry and thirsty as I was already, I knew that a night without water would also mean a night without sleep. I normally slept with a canteen within arms reach usually enjoying the precious liquid several times during the night whenever I awoke. This rest period I allowed myself thirty minutes. I wanted to give my muscles time to recuperate and my heart and breathing time to slow back to normal. As I relaxed the sun felt delightful warming my body. My skin and clothes were soaked from sweat. The temperature at this elevation was probably in the low 70s, yet I shivered when the breeze caressed me. The efficiency of the body's

cooling system amazed me, but now it was my enemy robbing me of precious life sustaining water.

The human condition is full of paradoxes. It is tough and hardy, normally able to suffer great abuse, yet fragile when lacking water or air or experiencing loss of blood. My situation changed dramatically from care and problem-free in the morning to desperate in the afternoon. As I lay looking up at the beautiful scenery and enjoying the warmth of the sun it was easy to put the problem out of mind momentarily. A bee buzzed curiously around my head until it realized this hunk of flesh offered nothing to enhance its existence. The buzzing moved away until it could no longer be heard. A couple of squirrels raced round and round and up and down a tree chattering loudly then quietly, oblivious to the stranger in their midst. Calm, peaceful and relaxing moments like these were few and far between back home in the "rat race". I dozed off momentarily, but awoke far too soon, coughing from a much too dry throat. It was okay because my half hour was more than past and it was time to load up and head out.

I was once again refreshed but the trail was as hideously steep as before. My plan for the moment was to go as slow as necessary but not to sit or lay down until the trail leveled off. If I had to stop to catch my breath and cool down it would be done while standing with the emphasis on *keep moving*. It was take three steps, stop, catch up with oxygen deficiency, take three more steps. At least this way my uphill pace would be steady and I wouldn't breath out of my mouth. My body was trying to hog all the attention so I put my mind

on other tasks to keep it from concentrating on the pain and difficulty at hand.

I thought of White Creek and jumping into the cold, clear, deep pools of water.

How refreshing it had been, how beautiful and invigorating. How I wished I had

just a little of that water with me now. Time to move the mind on. How

wonderful it would be to be out of the mountains and walk into a Pizza Hut all-

you-can-eat (and drink) lunch buffet. To fill a plate heaping with Caesar Salad

and cottage cheese and potato salad and sit down to begin feasting. To start

into a plate piled high with steaming hot meat-lovers delight, thick crust pizza.

One bite, filling my mouth with that cheese and meat flavor and pulling the

pizza away while the cheese hangs on in a long string. To chew that luscious

food, enjoy the delicious flavor and texture of pizza and to actually feel

uncomfortably full. Enough of those thoughts until I could make it a reality.

The suffering of thirst, the struggle to keep putting one foot in front of

the other was intense. There were other ways to deal with the current

dilemma. I could turn around and hike back to the last water source. It was

steep downhill most of the way. It would be a much easier trip than the

present one. My mind would never allow that solution as long as there was

breath and strength in this body. The obstacle before me was the most

difficult I had tackled in ages but I was sure I would succeed. After all, I had

unseen help even if it seemed He wasn't going to make things easier on me. It

was my challenge. How would I feel if at my beck and call He simply carried me to my destination? Even though at this moment it was what I thought I wanted, how would I feel looking back while enjoying a cold drink and pizza from the air conditioned comfort of a Pizza Hut? I would feel robbed of a challenge! As tough as this battle was right now, if the challenge was removed I would be desperately disappointed and always doubtful not knowing for sure if I could have overcome the obstacles. Sure, right now at this moment I thought I wanted to see divine intervention. But later I would be immensely angry to have failed or at least not know if I would have been able to succeed. These thoughts gave me the energy and anger or adrenaline to push on with renewed vigor. I was going to persevere until I made it. This trial was of my making after all.

The eternal minutes passed into hours, as my miserably slow steps became miles over the protest of my aching body and mind. Then ahead I saw the sign and the intersection with the Crest Trail! It instantly dawned on me that this was the trail where I had scared the eagle when my journey was just beginning. I was only a mile from the spring and it was even a fairly level mile. I sat and rested and gave thanks as my spirit soared. A mile on a level trail was nothing. I had succeeded. Though little had changed, the pain and dehydration already seemed a distant memory. The last five hours had seemed like weeks of torture yet I had traversed only four miles. Having hiked slower than one mile per hour made me feel puny and weak until I put it in perspective. I had carried fifty pounds four miles up nearly 3,000' of mountain. This was an accomplishment that might have killed me had it happened on my first day before the strenuous exercise toughened and strengthened my muscles and lungs.

There is little in life as exhilarating as overcoming a major challenge. Pushing oneself beyond what we think we can bear creates a better, stronger person. Can spirit beings experience anything comparable? Not having a limited physical body, unable to tire and feel pain, not needing oxygen and water, spirit beings must not be able to comprehend our fears, physical obstacles, accomplishments or challenges. Maybe the reason we will some day rule angels is because we have so much to overcome. If we can succeed in this life we will have a richer experience, deeper understanding, greater compassion, more appreciation. Our physical weaknesses and limitations give us greater strength and potentially make us superior beings spiritually.

Water dripping out of rocks at nearly 11,000 feet elevation is an amazing phenomenon at any time but when you are cotton mouthed thirsty, and practically dehydrated, the sight is one that causes song and praise to burst forth. I was pumped when I walked the quarter mile back to Hummingbird Saddle with canteens full of precious cold water. My prayers this night were longer and more enthusiastic than normal. Thanksgiving and praise were in order and thanksgiving and praise were joyfully offered.

As I lay on the ground in my sleeping bag looking up at the beautiful, bright, clear sky full of shining jewels I was full of peace and contentment thinking of the past eleven days' experiences. I was happy that tomorrow I would be back at the car and not many hours from food prepared by someone else and actually served to me. I would be able to simply ask for anything my taste buds desired and it would be cheerfully brought out and placed in front of me with no effort on my part. I wouldn't have to start a fire or clean up the utensils and I could eat as much as I wanted. I would once again have use for those paper bills that had been as useless as keys on this trip. Sadness at leaving this magnificent, awe inspiring place was tempered with anticipation of seeing loved ones and getting back to the world I normally inhabited. In a few weeks this place would be only a fond memory but the life changing experience would be part of me forever.

Epilogue

A backpacking experience is best enjoyed with a small group. The opportunities to talk and discuss familiar and unusual sights are frequent, numerous and enlightening. It affords the ability to get to know members of the group far more intimately than typical daily interactions ever do. One's strengths and weaknesses are revealed, camaraderies are developed, and each person's true spirit shines through. Whenever possible I backpack with friends and highly recommend it for everyone. But on the rare occasion that no one else is able to go along, I break the cardinal rule because as no wise old philosopher I know once said, "To backpack is to live" or was it "What is life without backpacking?"

"Thanks for reading! If you enjoyed this book or found it useful I'd be very grateful if you'd post a short review on Amazon. Your support really does make a difference and I read all the reviews personally so I can get your feedback and make this book even better.

Thanks again for your support!"